EVOLVE

WORKBOOK

Carolyn Clarke Flores and Michele Lewis

5 B

CAMBRIDGE
UNIVERSITY PRESS

CAMBRIDGE
UNIVERSITY PRESS

University Printing House, Cambridge CB2 8BS, United Kingdom

One Liberty Plaza, 20th Floor, New York, NY 10006, USA

477 Williamstown Road, Port Melbourne, VIC 3207, Australia

314–321, 3rd Floor, Plot 3, Splendor Forum, Jasola District Centre, New Delhi – 110025, India

103 Penang Road, #05–06/07, Visioncrest Commercial, Singapore 238467

Cambridge University Press is part of the University of Cambridge.

It furthers the University's mission by disseminating knowledge in the pursuit of education, learning and research at the highest international levels of excellence.

www.cambridge.org
Information on this title: www.cambridge.org/9781108411950

First published 2020

20 19 18 17 16 15 14 13 12 11 10 9 8 7 6 5 4 3 2

Printed in Great Britain by CPI Group (UK) Ltd, Croydon CR0 4YY

A catalogue record for this publication is available from the British Library

ISBN 9781108405331 Student's Book
ISBN 9781108405119 Student's Book A
ISBN 9781108409261 Student's Book B
ISBN 9781108405348 Student's Book with Practice Extra
ISBN 9781108405133 Student's Book with Practice Extra A
ISBN 9781108409278 Student's Book with Practice Extra B
ISBN 9781108409070 Workbook with Audio
ISBN 9781108408813 Workbook with Audio A
ISBN 9781108411950 Workbook with Audio B
ISBN 9781108405195 Teacher's Edition with Test Generator
ISBN 9781108410748 Presentation Plus
ISBN 9781108412056 Class Audio CDs
ISBN 9781108408004 Video Resource Book with DVD
ISBN 9781108414500 Full Contact with DVD
ISBN 9781108411561 Full Contact with DVD A
ISBN 9781108414210 Full Contact with DVD B
Additional resources for this publication at www.cambridge.org/evolve

CONTENTS

7.1 WORTHY HELPERS

1 VOCABULARY: Positive experiences

A Complete the sentences with the words in the box.

beneficial	contribution	devote	~~difference~~	honor	influence
pleasure	reassure	satisfaction	use	value	worthwhile

1 I started a recycling program at school because I wanted to make a _____difference_____.
2 The kid next door is a good _____ on Kevin.
3 Some people _____ their lives to serving their family, friends, and neighbors.
4 I needed my mother to _____ me that everything would be fine once I started college.
5 It was an _____ to have someone like him speak to the students.
6 Maybe his advice will be of _____ to you when you're older.
7 Many people take _____ in helping others.
8 She made an important _____ to today's meeting.
9 I _____ his friendship more than I could ever say.
10 She feels that teaching is a _____ career.
11 I get more _____ out of cooking than I do out of eating.
12 Drinking a lot of water is _____ for our health.

2 GRAMMAR: Gerunds and infinitives after adjectives, nouns, and pronouns

A Match the sentence halves.

1	It's unusual	f	a to help us with the repairs in this house.
2	Latin is an interesting language	___	b starting a new subject in school.
3	Simon often wastes time	___	c being alone in a big noisy crowd.
4	She has places	___	d to help him with his homework.
5	Valeria always feels nervous	___	e to learn.
6	We need someone	___	f to see them at this type of restaurant.
7	Samuel asked someone in class	___	g to visit this summer.
8	It can be scary	___	h watching TV.

B   Complete each sentence with the gerund or infinitive form of the verb in parentheses ( ).

1   I spent a lot of time _____*trying*_____ different sushi restaurants while I was in Japan. (try)

2   We had _____ about whether to buy their house or not. (think)

3   Sometimes it's hard _____ the only boy in the classroom. (be)

4   We needed someone _____ us a ride to the train station. (give)

5   I felt nervous _____ for the airplane to take off. (wait)

6   It's not unusual _____ more than you have. (want)

7   My car needs _____ fixed before I can drive it back home. (be)

8   There are sites that are interesting _____ in this ancient city. (visit)

3   GRAMMAR AND VOCABULARY

A   (Circle) the correct verb to complete the sentences. Then add another sentence using the cues in parentheses.

1   A   I spent time *to see /* (*seeing*) my sick grandmother this weekend. (make a difference)

    B   *I think it really made a difference* _____ .

2   A   I think I need a teacher *to talk / talking* about my future goals. (reassure)

    B   _____ .

3   A   I didn't waste my time *explaining / to explain* it to them. (value)

    B   _____ .

4   A   It's common *testing / to test* a product first before putting it on the market. (beneficial)

    B   _____ .

5   A   They always have volunteers *to help / helping* them during a crisis. (devote their life to)

    B   _____ .

6   A   The charity always needs more people *to support / supporting* them. One way to do this is to give money. (make a contribution)

    B   _____ .

B   Use a gerund or infinitive to complete the sentences so that they are true for you.

1   I take great pleasure in _____ .

2   It's been beneficial _____ .

3   There's a lot of use in _____ .

4   I think it's worthwhile _____ .

5   I get a lot of satisfaction out of _____ .

BUYER'S REGRET

1 VOCABULARY: Making purchases

A Circle the correct meaning for each sentence.

1 I was silly to buy the expensive boots because I already have a closet full of them.

   a I regret the purchase.

   b I think the boots look ridiculous.

2 Our parents always help us to feel confident about doing things we don't think we can do.

   a Our parents convince us to do things.

   b Our parents encourage us to do things.

3 Mia has a lot of useful ideas that can help us solve these problems.

   a Mia's ideas are foolish.

   b Mia's ideas are practical.

4 My husband doesn't want me to buy the car because it is not a good value for the price.

   a He thinks the car is not worth the money.

   b He thinks the car does not have potential.

5 I hope the seminar will persuade you to sign up for French classes.

   a I hope the seminar will convince you.

   b I hope the seminar is practical.

6 Don't buy the cheapest shoes. They are not such good value.

   a I encouraged her to buy the cheapest shoes.

   b I urged her not to buy the cheapest shoes.

B Complete the sentences with the words and phrases in the box.

have appeal	have potential	look ridiculous
~~make financial sense~~	regretted the purchase	urged

1 It might _____make financial sense_____ to buy this when it's on sale.

2 We should take these costumes off before leaving the party, so we don't _____ walking home.

3 Several lawyers strongly _____ the parents to take further legal action.

4 These regions _____ for economic development.

5 The commercials _____ which will attract a lot of people to their website.

6 Javier bought an expensive table. After he paid the delivery fee, he _____ .

C **THINK CRITICALLY** What are some things that people may regret buying? Why might they regret their purchases?

_____

_____

_____

2 GRAMMAR: Infinitives after verbs with and without objects

A **Put the words in the correct order to make sentences.**

1 wanted / some of the repairs / she / to help / him / pay for / her

   She wanted him to help her pay for some of the repairs.

2 encouraged / she / for my business / to buy / a new computer / me

3 on time / needed / Alejandra / the project / to finish

4 online / she / to buy / likes / clothes

5 to come / always / my parents / urged / on time / home / us

6 want / tomorrow morning / the children / to sleep in

7 to / decided / so / he / to talk / a doctor / was sick / my brother

8 to travel / at night / she / not / alone / us / warned

3 GRAMMAR AND VOCABULARY

A (Circle) the correct infinitive and then write a phrase from exercises 1A and 1B to complete the conversation. **Watch your verb tense.**

1 A My friend encouraged me (to wear)/ wear an animal dress to the party.

   B Oh, no. You must have _____ *looked ridiculous* _____ .

2 A We plan *waiting / to wait* on buying a house until the prices go down.

   B Good idea. It _____ .

3 A My boss is very upset because I forgot *to tell / telling* him I was going on vacation today.

   B No wonder he's mad. That _____ .

4 A I tend *wearing / to wear* comfortable shoes over fashionable ones.

   B So, do I. I think it _____ .

5 A I'm sad *to see / seeing* that it sold. I was hoping to buy it.

   B Don't worry. It was _____ .

6 A We decided *getting / to get* a new front door before we sell the house.

   B That's a good idea. It will certainly _____ .

7.3 A GOOD BARGAIN

1 LISTENING

A 🔊 **7.01** **Listen to the conversation. Then write *T* (true) or *F* (false) next to the statements.**

1 Jorge doesn't want to accept Stella's first offer. _____

2 Stella thinks the rug is too expensive. _____

3 Stella doesn't buy the rug. _____

B 🔊 **7.01** **UNDERSTAND PERSUASIVE TECHNIQUES** **Listen to the conversation again. Check (✓) the techniques each person uses to get the best deal.**

Stella says she loves the color of the rug	☐
says she only has $250 to buy the rug	☐
says the rug is too small	☐
says the rug is not worth that much	☐
says she's bought many rugs at street markets before	☐
tells Jorge she'll look around for another rug	☐
Jorge points out that many customers get a lot of satisfaction out of the rugs he sells	☐
tells Stella he made the rug himself	☐
refuses to give stuff for free	☐
reassures Stella that $250 is a good price for the rug	☐
says someone else will buy the rug if Stella doesn't	☐
says he'll clean the stain on the rug for Stella	☐

2 CRITICAL THINKING

A **THINK CRITICALLY** **Why do some people feel nervous about buying things at a street market? What are some advantages and disadvantages of buying things at a street market instead of a store?**

_____

_____

_____

A Complete the conversations with the phrases in the box.
You can use the phrases more than once. Then decide which
conversation accepts an offer, and which rejects an offer.

a little on the high side	don't think it's worth that much
go any lower	got a deal
~~how much are you asking for it~~	I can't accept that
the best I can do	throw in some stuff for free
sounds fair enough	sorry, but no deal
would you be willing to accept	

1 A I love this chair. So, ¹ how much are you asking for it ?

  B I'm selling it for $100.

  A Oh, really? Hmmm. That's ² _____ . Can you ³ _____ ?

  B I can give it to you for $75.

  A ⁴ _____ $60 for it?

  B ⁵ _____ .

  A Oh, that's too bad. I guess I'll have to shop somewhere else.

2 A Is this the car you're selling? So,¹ _____ ?

  B I would like $5,000 for it.

  A I'm sorry, but ² _____ .

  B I'll ³ _____ .

  A Like what?

  B A tank of gas and new windshield wipers.

  A I'm sorry, but I ⁴ _____ .

  B OK, $4,200 is ⁵ _____ .

  A That ⁶ _____ .

B Read the situation. Write a conversation that accepts an offer or refuses an offer between the buyer and
the seller.

Situation: Mario is on vacation at a beach resort. He is approached by a woman selling necklaces for $45 each.
He really wants to buy one for his girlfriend, but he only wants to spend $30.

A ¹ _____

B ² _____

A ³ _____

B ⁴ _____

A ⁵ _____

B ⁶ _____

MONEY'S WORTH

1 READING

A **IDENTIFY MAIN POINTS** Read the article. Check (✓) the best summary.

a Spending money on yourself can increase happiness. ....

b Spending money on others can increase happiness. ....

c People who are wealthy should spend money on others. ....

SPENDING ON OTHERS COULD MAKE A DIFFERENCE IN YOUR LIFE

There's a Chinese saying that goes something like this: "If you want happiness for a day, do something for yourself. If you want happiness for a lifetime, do something for others." Many researchers believe these words of wisdom when it comes to how you spend money, once your basic needs are met, of course.

In related studies, researchers Elizabeth Dunn and Michael Norton noted in their book *Happy Money: The Science of Happier Spending* (2013) that people who spend their money on others seem to get more satisfaction than those who spend their money on themselves. Spending on those you care about, or even strangers, can boost overall happiness levels. But they do point out that happiness comes from spending money on others because you want to, not from spending it out of guilt or obligation.

In another study, the World Happiness Report (2019) revealed that there is a high level of unhappiness among Americans. It was reported that this could be due to people not spending enough of their money on others. Spending money on charities, or making donations, could make people happier. Just ask someone like Bill Gates. According to many, this billionaire is happy devoting his time and money to others. It's been said that he gets more pleasure in spending most of his billions on charities and scientific research than on personal luxuries.

The good news is you don't have to be wealthy to spend money on others. Buying someone a coffee, making a small contribution to a charity, or giving a few dollars to a homeless person could be worthwhile as it helps us communicate and connect with people. That warm, happy feeling you get every time you spend on others rather than on yourself might make a big difference to your level of happiness and overall well-being.

B **IDENTIFY SUPPORTING DETAILS** Read the article again. Answer the questions.

1 According to the article, what kind of spending makes people happier?

2 What do researchers Elizabeth Dunn and Michael Norton say about how to spend on others?

3 Why might many Americans be unhappy?

4 As mentioned in the article, what are some ways that we can spend money on others to make ourselves happier?

2 CRITICAL THINKING

A **THINK CRITICALLY** Besides personal happiness, think of other reasons why spending money on others could be positive in someone's life. In what ways do you spend money on yourself? What about on others? How do you feel when you spend money on others?

A Read part of an essay. What two arguments are given? What is the author's own opinion?

Can Money Buy Happiness?

Recently, there have been a number of articles about what makes people happy. Many authors argue that having enough money to buy the necessary things in life can be enough for people to be happy, while others believe that those things might not be enough.

Let's consider some arguments in favor of how having enough money for the basic things in life can make people happy. To begin with, happiness can be achieved if we have money to pay for shelter, food, and clothing. When people are able to buy these things, they don't have to worry about their families or themselves. One thing for sure is that money can give us a sense of … . For example, money can … . Furthermore, money can help us feel healthy. For instance, … . Overall, these things in life can certainly help us feel happy.

On the other hand, having only enough money for the basic things in life might not always bring happiness. For some people, happiness comes from having things that make them more comfortable. For instance, having money beyond what we need might make certain people feel … . In addition, some people are happy having things such as … . These things can make their life seem more valuable. However, if people don't have things in life such as … , then what good is having money?

Money might not always buy happiness. It's my opinion that money can't always buy the things that truly are important to the quality of our lives. We can't buy our health or our friends … .

B Read the essay again. Write ideas that could complete the essay.

CHECK AND REVIEW

Read the statements. Can you do these things?

UNIT 7	Mark the boxes. ☑ I can do it. [?] I am not sure. I can …	If you are not sure, go back to these pages in the Student's Book.
VOCABULARY	☐ describe positive experiences. ☐ talk about making purchases.	page 67 page 68
GRAMMAR	☐ use gerunds and infinitives after adjectives, nouns, and pronouns. ☐ use infinitives after verbs with and without objects.	page 67 page 69
LISTENING AND SPEAKING SKILLS	☐ understand persuasive techniques. ☐ use arguments to accept and reject an offer.	page 70 page 71
READING AND WRITING SKILLS	☐ identify main ideas and supporting details. ☐ write a for-and-against essay.	page 72 page 73

8.1   ANNOYING LITTLE THINGS

1   VOCABULARY: Describing neatness and messiness

A   **Complete the sentences with the phrases in the box.**

arrange them neatly	disorganized	fold sth	hang sth up
jumbled up	leave things all over the place	line up	organized
put away	put sth in alphabetical order	~~put sth in a pile~~	
tangled up	throw something in/on		

1 When you _____ put sth in a pile _____ , you position objects one on top of the other.

2 When you _____ , especially paper or cloth, you bend it so that it takes up less room.

3 When you _____ shoes, you put them in a neat row.

4 When a cord is twisted in an untidy mass, it is _____ .

5 When toys are mixed together untidily, they are _____ .

6 When you _____ dishes, you put them where they are usually kept.

7 When you _____ , you place it on a hanger or a hook.

8 When you _____ , you arrange it in the same order as the letters of the alphabet.

9 When you put something quickly and carelessly on a chair, you _____ it.

10 When you plan things carefully and keep things tidy, you are _____ .

11 When you put a group of objects in careful order, you _____ .

12 When you are not good at planning or organizing things, you are _____ .

13 When you _____ , they are spread out in a large area in a disorganized way.

2   GRAMMAR: Modal-like expressions with *be*

A   **Rewrite the sentences using the expressions in parentheses ().**

1 He is certain to be late because he cannot find his keys. (bound to)

   He is bound to be late because he cannot find his keys.

2 He's going to meet his friends at the train station. (about to)

3 The train is expected to leave at 4:10 p.m. (supposed to)

4 His friends are certain to be mad if he misses the train. (sure to)

5 When he got there, he was made to go to another platform. (forced to)

B Read the complaints that Tanya and Marco have about each other. (Circle) the correct modal to complete the sentences.

> It annoys me when I'm late for work. We are ¹*about to* / (*supposed to*) be at the train station at 8:00 a.m., but Tanya can never find her coat or shoes in the mornings. Since I don't want to be late again, I'm ²*bound to* / *forced to* put everything near the front door after she goes to bed at night. It annoys me that when I get home her things are ³*sure to* / *about to* be left all over the place again.

> He should talk! When we are ⁴*about to* / *sure to* leave in the morning, Marco always wants to wash the dishes first. We can never get to the train station on time. Sometimes, he's too organized. It really annoys me when I get home because he's ⁵*supposed to* / *bound to* be cleaning and putting my things away.

C **THINK CRITICALLY** Read the complaints again. Do you think it's reasonable for Tanya and Marco to be annoyed with each other? Give reasons why.

_____

_____

_____

D Complete the sentences so that they are true for you.
1 This week, I am due to _____.
2 I was about to _____, but
   _____.
3 The weather is sure to be _____ tomorrow.
4 When I was young, my parents forced me to _____.
5 When I'm older, I'm bound to be _____.

3 GRAMMAR AND VOCABULARY

A Write sentences with your own ideas using the word prompts.
1 forced to / leave things all over the place
   When I was young, my mother was forced to pick up the toys we left all over the place .
2 bound to / throw on
   _____.
3 supposed to / put away
   _____.
4 sure to / put in alphabetical order
   _____.
5 about to / tangled up
   _____.

1   VOCABULARY: Talking about progress

A   **Circle the correct meaning of each vocabulary word or phrase.**

1	as expected	did not happen as predicted	(happened as predicted)
2	with ease	without problems	with problems
3	smoothly	easily	with difficulty
4	efficiently	slowly and badly	quickly and well
5	little by little	slowly and gradually	quickly and rapidly
6	with difficulty	without problems	with problems
7	in my own time	when I am not working	when I am working
8	steadily	rapidly	gradually
9	successfully	achieving good results	achieving bad results
10	thoroughly	quickly	completely
11	at my own pace	at a speed comfortable to you	to do something slowly
12	effectively	with no results	with good results

B   **Complete the sentences with words or phrases from exercise 1A.**

1   We can't repair our house all at once, so we'll have to repair it _____little by little_____ .

2   _____ , he was late again for the meeting. He's always late.

3   If all goes _____ , we should arrive by nine o'clock.

4   I _____ enjoyed the performance tonight.

5   The medicine works more _____ if you take a hot drink after it.

6   Jorge finally finished his essay, but _____ .

7   She wasn't in any pain and won the 400-meter race _____ .

8   I like to make and sell wooden chairs _____ in the evenings and at weekends.

9   They are so organized. They run their business very _____ .

10   A number of patients have been treated _____ with the new drug.

11   Food prices have risen _____ over the years.

12   I studied English _____ at home. It was slower than taking classes, but less expensive.

2 GRAMMAR: Future forms

A **Underline** the verb phrase in each sentence that shows the future.

1 Eventually, <u>we'll be living</u> in our newly built home.

2 I don't think she's going to attend the event.

3 Sooner or later, she might want to go back to her home country.

4 In a few years, we'll be buying a new car.

5 This book won't fill you with joy, but it will give you some inspiration.

6 If my business doesn't run efficiently, I might hire more people.

7 I'm not going to her party unless she invites me herself.

8 This side project of mine is going to allow me to make some extra money.

B **Correct the mistake in each sentence.**

1 Next month, we're going ~~moving~~ to another area in the city.   _to move_

2 She'll be return from her trip very soon. _____

3 Eating too much candy won't be killing you, but it will hurt your teeth. _____

4 When you get there, you go to take the bus to their house. _____

5 Next week, we're going to be travel in Europe. _____

6 By the summer, they won't be make any more money from these hats. _____

7 I guess you will be feel tired after working in the sun all day. _____

8 This presentation is going take a long time, so let's get comfortable. _____

3 GRAMMAR AND VOCABULARY

A **Create sentences in the future form with your own ideas.**

1 as expected / technology in the future

   As expected, technology in the future will be changing all the time .

2 successfully / a side project

   _____ .

3 efficiently and effectively / my business

   _____ .

4 little by little / my future plans

   _____ .

5 in my own time / learn a new language

   _____ .

6 smoothly / getting more customers

   _____ .

B **THINK CRITICALLY** What are the pros of turning a side project into a business? What might be the cons?

_____

_____

_____

_____

_____

_____

8.3 THE LITTLE TOUCHES

1 LISTENING

A 🔊 **8.01** Listen to the conversation between two siblings, Sarah and Leo. Check (✓) the "little touches" they are planning for their grandma's birthday.

Bake her a cake ☐

Order pink balloons ☐

Order food from her favorite Greek restaurant ☐

Buy fancy napkins ☐

Have a fun theme ☐

Get a karaoke machine ☐

Play her favorite songs ☐

Tell people to dress like they did in the 50s ☐

B 🔊 **8.01** RECOGNIZE EMPHASIS Listen to the conversation again and <u>underline</u> the words which are emphasized. Write *C* for the words that show a contrasting idea.

1 I think we need to do something <u>really</u> special.

2 Hmmm, I'm not sure she would like that.

3 That's such a terrific idea!

4 Of course, I bet everyone will love that!

5 My house is such a mess.

6 How about we throw the surprise party in your apartment?

7 What a fabulous idea!

8 She likes the new Greek restaurant.

9 Grandma will be so happy.

10 Don't worry. It will.

11 That's such an awesome idea!

2 CRITICAL THINKING

A THINK CRITICALLY How might choosing a theme for a party or an event help make planning it easier? How might having a theme make it difficult to plan?

62

3 SPEAKING

A **Circle the correct words to complete the conversations.**

1 **A** What should we do for Sandra's retirement party? She's worked here for almost 20 years!

   B Going out for lunch always ¹(*goes* / *went*) over well for retirement parties.

   A Hmmm, I don't think that's a good way to ²(*have* / *approach*) it. One ³(*thing* / *way*) we could do is have it catered.

   B I ⁴(*know* / *bet*) everyone will love that!

2 **A** What should we do for Dunia's graduation? She's worked so hard to become a lawyer.

   B It never ¹(*hurts* / *goes*) to give her money.

   A Hmmm. Or another ²(*idea* / *thing*) we could do is take her on a vacation.

   B That's always ³(*good* / *worth*) considering.

3 **A** What should we do for John's birthday? He'll be turning 12 years old!

   B One ¹(*approach* / *thing*) we could do is take him to a movie.

   A Hmmm, I don't think that's a good way to ²(*consider* / *approach*) it. Having a party always ³(*goes* / *went*) over well.

   B That's such an awesome ⁴(*idea* / *approach*)!

B **Choose an idea for an event from the list below. Write a conversation between you and a friend who is helping you plan the event.**

- A dinner party to congratulate your husband on his big job promotion
- A going away party for your friends who are taking a trip around the world
- A New Year's Eve party
- A housewarming party to celebrate moving into your new house

A _____

B _____

A _____

B _____

1 READING

A IDENTIFY WRITER'S PURPOSE **Read the article. What's its purpose? Check (✓) the best statement.**

a To tell readers to be calm when they are in traffic. ....

b To advise readers why they shouldn't worry and complain about the small stuff. ....

c To warn readers that feeling stressed can weaken the immune system. ....

● ● ● ◁ ▷ 🔍 🏠

HOW DO YOU DEAL WITH THE LITTLE THINGS IN LIFE?

Are you one of those people who complain and worry about the small stuff? Well, don't. Scientists have recently discovered that people who worry and complain about the little annoyances in life may be putting their health at risk.

While there are some people who get through the small stuff—heavy traffic, miserable weather, or canceled dinner plans—with ease, there are those who react with anger or frustration. When these little challenges or difficulties arise, emotions are bound to rise, too. Our bodies react, but not in a good way.

Recent studies show that negative emotions can flood the bloodstream with stress hormones. These hormones are released into the body when it interprets danger or threat. When they do, it can decrease our energy levels, increase heart rate and blood pressure, and in some instances, slow down digestion and reproduction organs. If that's not enough, stress hormones can make the immune system weak, which can cause other illnesses in the body.

What can we do? Well, practice being calm. Meditate, find deep breathing exercises, or concentrate on happy, positive thoughts when things don't go smoothly. Visualize the road becoming free of traffic or that rainy day bringing sunshine. Calming the mind and imagining things will work out can improve our health, both physically and mentally.

It takes practice to be calm. But we need to train our brain to deal with strong emotions when something annoys or frustrates us. So, the next time something small irritates you, learn from it and take control of your reaction. Know that worrying over the little stuff will not only ruin your day, but will be sure to affect your health, too.

B Read the article again. What specific examples of why we shouldn't complain about the small stuff does the writer mention? What advice does the writer suggest?

2 CRITICAL THINKING

A THINK CRITICALLY **What situations might make people worry and complain about the "big stuff"? Think of three examples. Why might they worry about these things?**

_____

_____

_____

3 WRITING

A Read the complaint email. <u>Underline</u> the problem and how Mira would like the company to solve it.

To: Ms. Suzanne Castillo
From: Mira Kim

Dear Ms. Castillo,

I recently bought a $450 printer from your company. I made the purchase on December 17 and the receipt number is 294738. It was a present for my husband who needed a high-quality laser printer for his new business. However, this product is definitely not high-quality. When the printer was delivered, the box was damaged and the paper tray was broken. Also, the glass is scratched, so any copies that we make have lines on them. Finally, the printer is very slow. This is unacceptable and I would like a replacement printer.

I have attached a copy of my receipt to this email. I would like your company to collect the broken printer from my house and deliver a new one as soon as possible. I look forward to hearing from you in the next week.

Sincerely,

Mira Kim

B Read the email again. Choose an idea below and write a more polite email that describes the problem and how you would like the company to solve it. Use expressions like *I find*, *I feel*, *I believe*, or *I think* if you can.

> The couch you ordered is wobbly and uncomfortable.
>
> Your car is still making a loud noise after it was repaired by a mechanic.
>
> The hotel room was small and dirty.

CHECK AND REVIEW

Read the statements. Can you do these things?

UNIT 8	Mark the boxes. ✔ I can do it. ? I am not sure.	I can ...	If you are not sure, go back to these pages in the Student's Book.
VOCABULARY	☐	talk about neatness and messiness.	page 76
	☐	talk about progress.	page 78
GRAMMAR	☐	use modal-like expressions with *be*.	page 77
	☐	use future forms.	page 79
LISTENING AND SPEAKING SKILLS	☐	recognize emphasis.	page 80
	☐	suggest and show interest in ideas.	page 81
READING AND WRITING SKILLS	☐	identify the writer's purpose.	page 82
	☐	write a complaint letter.	page 83

1   VOCABULARY: Luck and choice

A   **Circle the correct word or phrase in each sentence.**

1   Finding work was difficult for Greg, but he finally got a *lucky break / chance encounter* with this company.

2   Samuel was *in the right place at the right time / wound up* because he found a good parking spot.

3   Little did I know that she would *wind up / not believe my luck* as my next manager.

4   She was *deliberate decision / fortunate* to be cheerful at work.

5   Is it just a *coincidence / chance encounter* that the person who ran the contest won first prize?

6   Mariana went through a *life-changing experience / lucky break* when she survived the accident.

7   You can't help but admire her *fortunate / determination* to reach her goal.

8   We made a *lucky break / deliberate decision* to spend less money on things we don't need.

9   The *path / fate* to success is not without difficulty.

10   They believed that *fate / deliberate decision* brought them together.

11   I couldn't *be fortunate / believe my luck* when I saw I had won the prize.

12   He didn't expect to meet his wife through a *coincidence / chance encounter* at a café.

B   **Imagine you are in these situations. What might you think? Complete the sentences with words from exercise 1A.**

1   You met a movie star in the elevator on your way down to the lobby.

I was in the _____*right*_____ place at the right time.

2   You found someone to help you sell your car.

It was very _____ I had him to help me.

3   You saw an old friend getting on the same plane as you.

It was a _____ that we were on the same plane.

4   You got a job with that big company right after you graduated.

It was a _____ that I got this great job so quickly.

5   You missed the bus so you wouldn't have to go to the meeting.

I made a _____ decision to miss the bus.

6   You studied the lines for weeks to get the acting part.

I had a lot of _____ to get this part.

2 GRAMMAR: Unreal conditionals

A **Put the words in the correct order to make sentences.**

1 would've shopped / I / expensive / if / somewhere else / expensive / knew / I / it was going to be

   If I knew it was going to be expensive, I would've shopped somewhere else .

2 study / would've failed the exam / if / I / hadn't helped me / I / he

   _____

   _____ .

3 would help / if / could / I / you / I

   _____

   _____ .

4 the Great Wall of China / I / if / anywhere in the world / could go / go see / I'd

   _____

   _____ .

5 all the cake / she'd / if / could reach the table / eat / our dog

   _____

   _____ .

6 Tamara might've gotten the job / if / hadn't been late / she

   _____

   _____ .

B **Circle the correct words to complete the sentences.**

1 If I'd known you were allergic to nuts, I _____ an apple pie.

   a would make   **(b)** would've made

2 If I hadn't _____ him when I did, I might not have become a dentist.

   a have met   **b** met

3 If you _____ a good friend, you'd help him with his exam.

   a were   **b** are

4 If Clara _____ busy, she might not have missed the call.

   a weren't   **b** hadn't been

5 I _____ figured this out if I hadn't read the instructions.

   a couldn't   **b** couldn't have

6 If the book had more action, I _____ be interested in reading it.

   a would   **b** will

3 GRAMMAR AND VOCABULARY

A **Use your own ideas to complete the unreal conditional sentences.**

1 I was fortunate. If I hadn't had met her, I _____ *wouldn't have gone travelling* .

2 Fate is what brought those two together. If she _____ ,
   she might not have _____ .

3 If she _____ , she'd be on a much better path then the one she's on now.

4 If I _____ , I'd have more determination to finish this project.

5 It was a coincidence. If Andres _____ , he wouldn't

   _____ .

9.2 WHY DID I DO IT?

1 VOCABULARY: Commenting on mistakes

A Find words in the word search.

h	a	r	d	b	c	h	j	u	i	b
u	a	b	z	k	j	l	c	o	n	a
r	c	u	f	l	w	b	m	p	c	w
r	v	d	k	i	a	s	n	k	o	k
y	e	j	y	t	t	i	m	i	m	w
d	u	m	b	s	c	l	d	c	p	a
h	f	o	g	e	h	l	o	k	e	r
i	w	v	w	q	r	y	t	p	t	d
x	g	e	h	f	a	u	l	t	e	q
f	u	n	n	y	w	c	u	s	n	r
u	n	f	o	r	t	u	n	a	t	e

awkward   dumb
fault   funny side
hard   hurry
incompetent   kick yourself
move   ~~silly~~
unfortunate   watch

B Complete the sentences with words from exercise 1A.

1 She showed little thought and judgment when she did that. It was a/an _____silly_____ mistake.

2 You are going to spill the milk if you don't _____ what you're doing.

3 Slow down. You're in too much of a/an _____ and you might make a mistake.

4 She found herself in a/an _____ situation when she forgot his name.

5 It's your own _____ that you lost your phone.

6 Lucky for me, he saw the _____ side of my error.

7 I learned the _____ way that going to school and working at the same time is challenging.

8 You know you'll _____ yourself if you forget to do it, so just do it now!

9 It was a bad _____ on my part for getting involved.

10 I know you need the money, but I think selling your favorite watch is a/an _____ thing to do.

11 She described him as being totally _____ at his job. He wasn't able to do the simplest task.

12 It was _____ that it rained during their game.

2 GRAMMAR: Wishes and regrets

A **Circle the correct words or phrases to complete the sentences. Then write if the sentences express present or past wishes.**

1 If only I *could* / *can* play the piano!   _present_

2 I wish I *taught* / *was teaching* in that other school again.   _____

3 I wish she *attends* / *had attended* the meeting.   _____

4 If only they *have* / *had* been more careful.   _____

5 I wish you *could* / *can* see the movie with us.   _____

6 If only someone *had taught* / *was teaching* me this when I was younger.   _____

7 I wish I *talked* / *had talked* to her yesterday.   _____

8 I wish I *was going* / *can go* on vacation with them.   _____

B **Complete the sentences with the correct form of the verbs in the box.**

go	grow	have	know	leave	perform	stop	~~study~~

1 I wish that I wasn't _____studying_____ art history.

2 If only someone had _____ her from getting up on the stage and embarrassing herself.

3 I wish I had _____ a little sister when I was growing up.

4 Tomas wishes he could _____ vegetables in his garden, but it is too small.

5 If only I _____ how to use a computer, I'd be doing a different job.

6 If only he _____ the house earlier, he wouldn't be stuck in a traffic jam.

7 I wish I could _____ on vacation with you next week, but I'm busy.

8 Amelia wishes she was _____ in the school play this year.

3 GRAMMAR AND VOCABULARY

A **For each conversation, comment on mistakes using the phrase in parentheses. Then finish each response with a wish or regret.**

1 **A** I made a big mistake yesterday when I quit my job.

  B _____That was a bad move_____ . (be a bad move)

  A You're right. I wish I _____hadn't quit my job_____ .

2 **A** I need to rush, or I'll be in trouble for being late.

  B _____ . (be your own fault)

  A You're right. If only my boss _____ .

3 **A** I think I'm going to demand a big pay raise.

  B _____ . (be a dumb thing to do)

  A You're right. I wish I _____ .

4 **A** I couldn't find my train ticket, so I had to buy another one.

  B _____ . (be unfortunate)

  A I know. If only I _____ .

5 **A** He needs more training. He cannot do what I ask him to do.

  B _____ . (be incompetent)

  A You're right. I wish he _____ .

6 **A** It was difficult starting my own business because I didn't get any help.

  B I bet _____ . (learn sth the hard way)

  A You're right. If only I _____ .

MY MISTAKE

1 LISTENING

A 🔊 9.01 **Listen to the conversation. Then write _T_ (true) or _F_ (false) next to the statements.**

1 Henry has an audition today.   F
2 Carmen made a lot of silly mistakes.   ....
3 Laura Medford was in a different room.   ....
4 Carmen tells Henry to leave his phone at home or in his car. ....
5 Laura Medford showed up at the office.   ....
6 Henry didn't notice Laura Medford at the coffee shop.   ....
7 Laura Medford spilled coffee all over the front of Henry's expensive pants. ....
8 Henry was told to come and do the audition again.   ....

B 🔊 9.01 **IDENTIFY FEELINGS** Listen to the conversation again. Circle the word that best describes Henry's feelings.

1 When Henry said his lines in front of his favorite actress, he felt …
   a cheerful   (b confused)   c calm

2 When his phone rang in the middle of the audition, he was …
   a amused   b sad   c annoyed

3 When Henry saw Laura Medford at the coffee shop, he was …
   a surprised   b calm   c angry

4 When Laura spilled coffee all over his expensive shirt, Henry was …
   a confused   b annoyed   c calm

5 When he was told to come and do the audition again, he felt …
   a cheerful   b annoyed   c amused

2 CRITICAL THINKING

A **THINK CRITICALLY** Why do you think it would be hard for some people to accept their mistakes? Think of how they might feel or what they might fear.

_____

_____

_____

_____

_____

3 SPEAKING

A (Circle) the correct word to complete the expressions of reassurances.

1 **A** Look at my hair. It's a mess!

   B It's not that *good /* (bad).

2 **A** I think I left my wallet on the table at the café.

   B We all make *mistakes / errors*.

3 **A** I didn't get the promotion I was expecting at work.

   B That's the way it *went / goes*.

4 **A** I'm upset that I broke my arm in the car accident last weekend.

   B It could have been *worse / better*.

5 **A** The vase broke when I accidentally dropped it.

   B You're not the only one who's *done / did* that.

6 **A** I'm so embarrassed that I forgot her birthday.

   B Don't worry. No one is *good / perfect*.

7 **A** If I don't find a job soon, I'll have to move out of this apartment.

   B It'll turn out all *wrong / right*.

8 **A** Well, it's done now. I can't go back and re-write the test.

   B You're right. There's no use in *crying / laughing* over spilled milk.

9 **A** I don't think they're going to call me back for a second interview.

   B What are you worrying *for / over*? It will be fine.

B **For each situation write an expression of reassurance and then give advice.**

1 **A** Oh, no. I got a terrible haircut!

   B 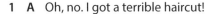 It's not that bad. It'll grow out soon.

2 **A** I lost one of the books I borrowed from my friend.

   B _____

3 **A** I feel so bad. I won't be able to make it to her party this weekend.

   B _____

4 **A** I failed my driving test.

   B _____

5 **A** I couldn't get tickets to the big concert this weekend.

   B _____

6 **A** I'm sorry, but I got the schedule all wrong. I think we missed the train.

   B _____

GOOD CONVERSATIONS

1 READING

A **MAKE PREDICTIONS** Read the title of the article. What do you think the writer means by "conversation flow"? Then read the article. Was your prediction correct?

HOME   NEWS   **BLOG**   SIGN IN

THE SECRET OF CONVERSATION FLOW

What makes conversations so special? Well, they all have something called *conversation flow*. Conversation flow happens when conversation is comfortable, effortless, and smooth. It's the way conversations are supposed to work.

Sometimes, conversation flow seems to happen automatically. You and your conversation partner get along and the conversation feels very friendly and natural. That's great when it happens, but what do you do when the conversation doesn't flow?

That's where the ideas of invitation and inspiration come in. An invitation is when you say something that lets your conversation partner clearly know it's her turn to speak. And when your partner says something to you that makes you want to speak, that's known as inspiration. Invitation and inspiration are the key ingredients of smooth, comfortable conversation. These conversational strategies keep the conversation flowing. Learn how to use them and you will have conversations free of awkward pauses and fake small talk.

> **Here's how it works:**
> Let's say that you and your friend Steve are chatting as you work.
> You ask, "How was your weekend?"
> Steve replies, "Oh, it was great. How was yours?"
> You reply, "It was fine."
> Steve says nothing and goes back to work.

What happened? Well, you didn't give Steve a clear invitation or a strong inspiration. Without either of those things, he didn't know what to say next (and perhaps was unsure if it was his turn to speak). So, he didn't respond. The conversation failed.

Without an invitation or an inspiration, your partner might not know what to say or whether to respond. That's why you want to make sure to offer invitations and inspirations to your partner in order to have a conversation flow.

B Read the article again. How do invitation and inspiration keep a conversation flowing?
What is an example of an invitation you could give Steve to keep the conversation going?

2 CRITICAL THINKING

A **THINK CRITICALLY** Do you know anyone who is good at conversation? What kind of things do they talk about, and what conversational strategies do they use?

A **Read the article. Summarize the tips it gives. What is the easiest tip to do in the article? What about the hardest?**

HOW TO START A CONVERSATION WITH THREE BODY LANGUAGE TIPS 🔍

BODY LANGUAGE TIPS

Using body language to help you start a conversation can lead to great conversation. You do not have to say much because just a look or a movement can be beneficial.

The following shows the main points of body language you should be aware of when you want to start a conversation.

EYE USE:

We can learn all about a person through their eyes. Your eyes can say many things and sometimes you may be unaware of what your eyes are saying. Be careful not to let your eyes say you are bored and are not listening.

BODY MOVES:

The way you move your hands, arms, feet, and head can say many things. Crossing your arms, tapping your foot rapidly, or putting your hands on your hips can all say things that might seem negative. Always be aware of what your body is saying.

FACIAL EXPRESSIONS:

Smiling can say more than words so be aware of your facial expressions at all times. You may frown and be unaware of it. Facial expressions can often be misunderstood if you give someone a serious look. They may think you do not like them.

Just make sure you are using the rest of your body to speak as well, and your facial expressions should come across clearly. Your eyes, body, and face can carry on a whole conversation for you.

B **Read the article again. Think of tips or go online for ideas about how to end a conversation. Write an article that gives at least three tips. Include a title, headings for each tip, and advice / explanations under each heading. Remember to use parallel structure in lists.**

_____

_____

_____

_____

CHECK AND REVIEW

Read the statements. Can you do these things?

UNIT 9	Mark the boxes. ☑ I can do it. ⃞? I am not sure. I can …	If you are not sure, go back to these pages in the Student's Book.
VOCABULARY	☐ use expressions for luck and choice. ☐ talk about mistakes.	page 86 page 89
GRAMMAR	☐ use unreal conditionals. ☐ describe wishes and regrets.	page 87 page 89
LISTENING AND SPEAKING SKILLS	☐ reassure someone about a problem. ☐ use expressions of reassurance correctly.	page 90 page 91
READING AND WRITING SKILLS	☐ make predictions. ☐ write an article giving tips.	page 92 page 93

10.1 ARE WE UNIQUE?

1 VOCABULARY: Describing characteristics

A **Complete the sentences with the words in the box.**

build	characteristic	feature
female	gender	individual
likeness	look	look-alike
male	~~match~~	similarity

1 He was a perfect _____match_____ to Luisa's outgoing personality.

2 A big nose is a typical _____ in her family.

3 They have the same _____. Their hair is very similar and so are their clothes.

4 It's more important to be a/an _____ than to copy everyone else.

5 Does this test show the _____ of the baby?

6 Her favorite _____ has always been her thick and curly hair.

7 I can see the _____ between you and your father.

8 She was voted the best _____ country singer in the world.

9 She has a slim _____ just like her mother.

10 Jorge is a twenty-five-year old _____ with dark hair and blue eyes.

11 When I look at you, there's a definite family _____ around the eyes.

12 She's a Marilyn Monroe _____ with her blond hair and pretty smile.

B **Answer the questions with your own information.**

1 What kind of look did you have when you were younger?

_____

2 What are some of your family's characteristics?

_____

3 Have you ever been told you're a look-alike for someone famous? If so, who?

_____

4 What is your favorite feature? What is your least favorite?

_____

C **THINK CRITICALLY What are some common reasons people change their facial features to avoid looking older? Do you think this is a good idea? Why or why not?**

_____

_____

_____

2 GRAMMAR: Gerunds after prepositions

A Complete the sentences with the correct form of the verbs in the box. Then <u>underline</u> the verb and the preposition.

~~build~~	exercise	go	have
pay	understand	wear	win

1 We plan on _____building_____ a new addition at the back of our house.
2 I often wonder about the possibility of _____ back to school.
3 She was concerned about _____ surgery next week.
4 Antonio and his wife did not like the idea of _____ the extra fee.
5 He's always succeeded in _____ games of chess.
6 Have you thought about _____ a watch? You're always losing track of time.
7 What are the benefits of _____ daily?
8 The experiment resulted in _____ more about the cancer drug.

B Rewrite the sentences by putting the verbs in parentheses in the correct place.

1 He succeeded in more about his team. (learn)
   He succeeded in learning more about his team.

2 What are the risks of eights cups of coffee a day? (drink)
   _____

3 We really like the idea of him to visit us this summer. (come)
   _____

4 Martha and her husband were concerned about home in the heavy rain. (drive)
   _____

5 Christopher wondered about the possibility of a long vacation. (take)
   _____

6 We plan on this project by the end of the week. (finish)
   _____

3 GRAMMAR AND VOCABULARY

A Complete the sentences with a gerund and your own ideas.

1 I never plan on _____ my facial features because _____ .
2 I sometimes think about _____ my look so I can _____ .
3 The risks of _____ to change your build are _____ .
4 The idea of _____ a look-alike somewhere in the world is _____ .
5 Some benefits of _____ a female might be _____ .

YOU, THE CUSTOMER

1 VOCABULARY: Describing research

A Complete the sentences with one of the word pairs from the box. Write *N* (noun) or *V* (verb) to show how each word is used in the sentence.

analyze/analysis	assess/assessment	calculate/calculation	demonstrate/demonstration
~~examine/examination~~	identify/identification	survey/survey	

1 a They need to _____examine_____ the chemical content in the metal.   V

   b Once the data is collected, there will be a/an _____examination_____ of it.   N

2 a Let me give you a/an _____ on how this works.

   b He wanted to _____ to her how it works.

3 a They had to show their _____ before entering the building.

   b The research will be used to _____ training needs.

4 a They collect the data and _____ the store profits.

   b If their _____ is wrong, they have to collect new data.

5 a It's too early to _____ if the product will be successful.

   b Her _____ of the production cost was completely inaccurate.

6 a A recent _____ showed that teenagers prefer to shop online.

   b The researchers had to _____ two age groups for their report.

7 a Simon's team had to _____ ways to re-route heavy traffic.

   b This part of the project still needs a complete _____ .

2 GRAMMAR: Causative verbs

A **Complete the sentences with the correct form of the verb in parentheses.**

1   Working at night allows him _____to go_____ (go) to school during the day.

2   The school lets parents _____ (know) if their child needs help.

3   You need to protect your identity from _____ (be) stolen online.

4   Computerization should enable them _____ (reduce) staffing costs.

5   If you wait here, we will have someone _____ (collect) it for you.

6   A system failure can cause everyone _____ (panic).

7   It's important to keep this information from _____ (reach) your senior staff.

8   Our manager sometimes makes us _____ (stay) late on the weekends.

9   Unfortunately, her sprained ankle prevents her from _____ (drive).

10 They put up barriers on the highway to stop cars from _____ (enter).

B **Check (✓) the correct sentences. Correct the incorrect sentences.**

1   Online shopping allows people ~~having~~ *to have* more time to themselves. ☐

2   Security guards prevent people from stealing items from the store. ☑

3   Having a good marketing strategy causes people wanting to buy more. ☐

4   Something must be done to stop them from arguing. ☐

5   Is this something they make all employees doing after their training? ☐

6   The new procedure has everyone to sign in first before their shift. ☐

7   The phone app lets you to know how much you have spent in the store. ☐

8   Georgina's shoes enabled her walking comfortably around the mall. ☐

3 GRAMMAR AND VOCABULARY

A **Circle the correct word and then complete the sentences with your own ideas.**

1   When people *calculate* / *calculation* their yearly budgets, it keeps
    _____them from spending too much money_____ .

2   *Analyzing* / *analysis* shopping trends allows
    _____ .

3   Using fake *identify* / *identification* can prevent
    _____ .

4   *Demonstrate* / *demonstrating* a new product on TV lets
    _____ .

5   Industry *surveys* / *survey* enables
    _____ .

6   *Assess* / *assessing* a product and its reviews makes
    _____ .

7   The *examine* / *examination* of people selling their products online has
    stopped some _____ .

1 LISTENING

A 🔊 **10.01** Listen to Anton talk about two jobs. What are they? How does he feel about them?

B 🔊 **10.01** **LISTEN FOR CONTRASTING IDEAS** Listen to the conversation again. Are Anton's ideas about the research company (R) or the sales company (S)? Which job does he like most? Which job would you choose?

1 Everyone looked happy there.   S
2 The work is similar to my current job.   _____
3 I'll be able to walk to work.   _____
4 I can make good money.   _____
5 I'd be responsible for a lot of the research.   _____
6 I'd use my sales skills.   _____
7 The pay isn't great.   _____
8 It'll be long hours.   _____
9 I'll learn more.   _____

2 CRITICAL THINKING

A **THINK CRITICALLY** How can you tell by looking at a company online that it would be a good place to work? Think of three important things that you would look for.

_____

_____

_____

_____

A **Complete the phrases with a word in the box.**

far	funny	gut	hunch
~~impression~~	judging	see	strikes

1 A You look happy today.

 B I get the _____impression_____ that everything went well at the meeting last night.

2 A Sandra still hasn't shown up to work.

 B I have a _____ feeling that she might not come in at all.

3 A Michael doesn't seem himself lately.

 B I have a _____ that he's going to quit soon.

4 A She left a big mess in the kitchen this morning.

 B _____ by appearance, she must've been in a rush.

5 A Their house is so big!

 B What _____ me about their house is that even though it's big, it still feels cozy.

6 A It's dark and there are no cars parked outside.

 B As _____ as I can tell, the restaurant is closed.

7 A She looks good in that dress.

 B From what I can _____, she's on a new diet.

8 A The technology company is doing very well.

 B My _____ feeling is that more people will apply to work here.

B **Look at the photos. Give your impressions about the two places. Use some of the expressions from exercise 3A.**

1

Restaurant 1

1 _____

Restaurant 2

2 _____

2

Beach 1

1 _____

Beach 2

2 _____

3

Workplace 1

1 _____

Workplace 2

2 _____

10.4 A PROFESSIONAL PROFILE

1 READING

A **How can a company make more money with a professional profile? Read the article. Were your ideas the same as those in the article?**

WRITE A COMPANY PROFILE THAT WINS BUSINESS

An attractive company profile is a great way to get potential customers to buy from you. Here are a few tips that will help you write the perfect profile.

1 Think about what customers want to know and adjust your content accordingly

Content is often based on what the company thinks their potential clients want to know. Before you prepare your document, you need to understand exactly what your potential clients would want to know about you.

2 Gather feedback

If you don't have a company profile, talk to the clients you already have, your friends, or your family. Ask them what questions they have about your products or services and try to provide the answers when you create the profile.

3 Update your current profile

If you already have a company profile, ask a few clients for their honest feedback on it. Think about the questions you are most frequently asked by your customers. These questions point to issues you'll need to address when you update your profile.

4 Use images

A lot of companies don't use images in their company profile, and this is a missed opportunity. If you're including information on the business owner and staff members, put photos next to their profiles. This helps to build a connection between the company and the client. You may also consider including a photo of your building or office.

5 Strengthen your brand

A company profile can be used to outline and reinforce what your business is about and establish your identity in the marketplace. Don't forget to use your logo and company colors. This will ensure that your customers will always know who you are. It also makes your profile look more professional.

B **TAKE NOTES** Read the article again. Take notes about each of the five points. Then summarize each point with a sentence.

2 CRITICAL THINKING

A **THINK CRITICALLY** Imagine you're a small business owner. If you want to win more business, what questions would you ask your customers?

_____

_____

_____

A   Read an excerpt from a company profile. <u>Underline</u> the language that is too informal. Is there any language that is considered too formal?

👤 COMPANY PROFILE

Write Design is a self-publishing company for the young and old, and everyone in between! Write Design makes it super easy for you to design, publish, and promote your book. You can probably sell a lot of the professional-quality printed books and eBooks that we will make for you.

WD was founded by Liza Demetria in 2012. She is an author herself. She is working with a team of designers and media experts who share a passion for helping people bring their stories to life. Write Design authors have created a ton of books using their collection of book-making tools. A new book is created almost every minute! They are based in New York with offices in London …

B   **USE PROFESSIONAL LANGUAGE**   Write a better version of the company profile in exercise A using more professional language. Add more details using ideas from the box or some of your own.

- She has over 10 years of publishing experience.
- She has worked for one of the biggest publishing companies in the world.
- She started writing at the age of five and learned from her grandmother who wrote a bestseller.
- She knows how tough the publishing industry is.
- Millions of Write Designs books have been sold on Amazon.
- Books are her business.

CHECK AND REVIEW

Read the statements. Can you do these things?

UNIT 10	Mark the boxes. ✔ I can do it. ? I am not sure. I can …	If you are not sure, go back to these pages in the Student's Book.
VOCABULARY	☐ people's characteristics. ☐ customer research.	page 98 page 100
GRAMMAR	☐ use gerunds after prepositions. ☐ use complements of verbs describing cause and effect.	page 99 page 101
LISTENING AND SPEAKING SKILLS	☐ listen for contrasting ideas. ☐ give your impressions.	page 102 page 103
READING AND WRITING SKILLS	☐ take notes. ☐ write a professional profile.	page 104 page 105

UNIT 11 REALLY?

11.1 FAKE!

1 VOCABULARY: Describing consumer goods

A **Circle** the correct meaning of each vocabulary word.

1 fake
- **a** an object that is made to look real or valuable
- **b** an object that is real or valuable

2 genuine
- **a** real, exactly what it appears to be
- **b** not real, not what it appears to be

3 imperfect
- **a** in perfect condition
- **b** damaged, has problems

4 authentic
- **a** real, true, or what people say it is
- **b** not real, false, not what people say it is

5 legal
- **a** not allowed by the law
- **b** allowed by the law

6 deadly
- **a** likely to cause death
- **b** unlikely to cause death

7 fireproof
- **a** able to be damaged by fire
- **b** unable to be damaged by fire

8 illegal
- **a** allowed by the law
- **b** not allowed by the law

9 sophisticated
- **a** made in a complicated way
- **b** made in an uncomplicated way

10 counterfeit
- **a** made to look like the real thing
- **b** made to look better than the real thing

11 original
- **a** related to a first or real product
- **b** related to copies of a real product

12 second-rate
- **a** cheaply made
- **b** well made

13 inferior
- **a** not as good as something else
- **b** just as good as something else

2 GRAMMAR: Passive forms

A **Underline the passive form in each sentence.**

1 These watches <u>are not always made</u> of quality material.

2 It's unlikely that the company will be stopped from producing these cheap products.

3 Two pink handbags were sold in the store last week.

4 Counterfeit watches were discovered while they were being sold on the streets.

5 Nothing is going to be sold by the athletic company this year.

6 The original painting was created by Sergio.

B **Rewrite the sentences using the correct form of the verbs in parentheses.**

1 The shoes _____ *are made* _____ by a small, Italian company. (make)

2 Our house _____ by a professional company next year. (renovate)

3 The little dog _____ in her oversized handbag. No one saw it. (carry)

4 Instructions _____ to you in the next few days. (sent)

5 The operation was a success. All the counterfeit money _____ by the police. (collect)

6 Illegal copies of the movies _____ by many of the stores. (sell)

7 The store is closing. Everything _____ at half price.(sell)

8 The problem is that second-rate items _____ to last long. (not design)

3 GRAMMAR AND VOCABULARY

A **Complete the sentences with your own ideas. Use passive forms.**

1 The genuine leather shoes _____ *were being sold at a much higher price* _____ .

2 Delicious food _____ at the authentic Italian restaurant.

3 Deadly chemicals _____ to make the jeans.

4 Sophisticated counterfeits _____ all over the internet.

5 It's unlikely that imperfect t-shirts _____ at the music festival.

6 Illegal copies of the artist's drawings _____ .

7 A waterproof and fireproof product _____ .

8 The fake gold necklaces _____ .

INTERNET TALES

1 VOCABULARY: Degrees of truth

A Circle the correct words to complete the sentences.

1 If you don't tell the truth, you're being *dishonest* / *honest*.

2 When you tell a lie to stop someone from being hurt, you tell a *suspicious* / *white* lie.

3 If people believe stories about something that actually never happened, then they fell for a *hoax* / *misinformation*.

4 A story or statement that's not true but is often repeated, and believed by many to be true, is an urban *legend* / *fact*.

5 When something is not completely correct, it is *accurate* / *inaccurate*.

6 When something is not real, it is *false* / *biased*.

7 If people feel that they can trust you, they call you *controversial* / *trustworthy*.

8 When you make something seem more important than it really is, it has been *exaggerated* / *misleading*.

9 You're *misleading* / *suspicious* when something doesn't seem right.

10 When a story could be true but might be invented, it is a *rumor* / *white lie*.

11 Something is *controversial* / *misinformation* when it causes disagreement and discussion.

12 If you like or dislike a person based on personal opinions, you are *suspicious* / *biased*.

13 It's *misinformation* / *controversial* when information is wrong or intended to deceive.

14 If a reporter uses a photo that suggests something that is not true, then the photo is *inaccurate* / *misleading*.

15 When something is exact and correct, it's *exaggerated* / *accurate*.

2 GRAMMAR: Passives with modals and modal-like expressions; passive infinitives

A Complete the sentences with *be* or *to be*.

1 Misleading stories shouldn't _____ *be* _____ discussed on the news.

2 This new smartphone seems _____ the best thing since sliced bread.

3 That type of news has _____ stopped from reaching the students.

4 This story is a hoax and shouldn't _____ believed.

5 She didn't expect _____ given an award for her news stories.

6 This report needs _____ done by this afternoon.

7 That type of work couldn't _____ done by one person.

8 I didn't want _____ thought of as a dishonest person, so I told the truth.

B **Complete the sentences with a modal or modal-like expression from the box. Use the correct verb tense.**

could	expect	have	must
~~need~~	seem	should	want

1 All news stories _____ need _____ to be checked.
2 They didn't _____ their story to spread as quickly as it did.
3 All the information _____ be collected and recorded first.
4 You _____ better listen to him or you'll be fired from your job.
5 We _____ be given directions for how to use this machine. It's complicated.
6 This _____ to be an important issue these days.
7 Future problems _____ be avoided if you address these issues now.
8 Jenna didn't _____ to be part of our team anymore.

C THINK CRITICALLY **What do you think spreads faster: facts or lies? Give reasons why.**

_____
_____
_____
_____
_____

3 GRAMMAR AND VOCABULARY

A **Write a sentence using the prompts and a word in the box. Use the passive forms with modals or modal-like expressions.**

~~accurate~~	false	hoax	misleading	rumor	trustworthy

1 only / information / report / news channel
   Only accurate information should be reported on a news channel.
2 story / tell / reporters
   _____
3 publish / stop / magazines
   _____
4 stories / research / source
   _____
5 information / check / report
   _____
6 dangerous / avoid / penalty
   _____

BELIEVE IT OR NOT ...

1 LISTENING

A 🔊 **11.01** **UNDERSTAND IMPORTANT DETAILS** **Listen to Chris and Adam talk about a possible hoax. Check (✓) the points people make to argue that the moon landing was fake.**

1 The American flag was waving, but there's no atmosphere on the moon. ☐

2 There isn't a big hole where the jet engine lifted off the moon. ☐

3 The moon reflects light from the sun. ☐

4 There were suspicious shadows and other light sources. ☐

5 Stars in the background cannot be seen when photographs were taken. ☐

6 The flag hangs completely limp in space when he steps away from it. ☐

7 The moon's atmosphere wouldn't have changed. ☐

B 🔊 **11.01** **Listen to the conversation again. Complete the sentences with a number from the box.**

21	billions	hundred	seven	ten	thirty

1 I heard that _____ percent of Americans now believe that the United States never went to the moon.

2 People talked about the American flag that was planted on the moon on July _____ , 1969.

3 The moon's atmosphere is something like _____ trillion times less dense than Earth's atmosphere.

4 There are _____ of stars in space.

5 The moon reflects about _____ percent of the light from the sun.

6 Over a _____ trustworthy scientists showed that this point, as well as the other points, were easily proven false.

2 CRITICAL THINKING

A **THINK CRITICALLY** **Which are more believable – the arguments for or against the moon landing? Give reasons why.**

_____

_____

_____

3 SPEAKING

A   Circle the correct word and then write *B* (Belief), *S* (Some belief), or *D* (Disbelief) beside each expression.

1   **A**   By 2030, everyone will be able to scan using their eyes.

    B   There's no *truth* / *right* in that.   D

2   **A**   I love to watch scary movies.

    B   Really? I've never watched one in my entire life, *believe* / *like* it or not.

3   **A**   Did you hear the story about the woman with three heads?

    B   You're so funny! *Tell* / *don't tell* me another one.

4   **A**   Eating only green vegetables can actually reverse the signs of aging.

    B   Hmmm. I find that *easy* / *hard* to believe.

5   **A**   So, that computer virus they warned us about was a hoax?

    B   Yes, I'm absolutely *positive* / *right* it was.

6   **A**   Did you hear about the new drug that can cure all diseases?

    B   Yeah, *wrong* / *right*!

7   **A**   She takes the subway to work every day because it's fast.

    B   That's partly *true* / *false*. But she also doesn't like the bus.

8   **A**   This story says that he lost his fortune because he was careless.

    B   There's probably some *truth* / *belief* in that.

B   **Express belief or disbelief about the rumors using the expressions from exercise 3A.**

1   Did you hear the rumor about <u>spaghetti</u> growing on <u>trees</u>?

    I did. There's no truth to it. Spaghetti is not a fruit or a nut.

2   Did you hear the rumor about an asteroid destroying Earth next year?

3   Do you think that dogs will really be able to talk one day?

4   I heard a rumor that people might soon be able to live to 150.

5   Drones are being used to find people lost at sea, believe it or not.

6   Someone said that by 2030, there won't be any clean water left in the world.

CONVINCE ME

1 READING

A **Read the article about diamonds. How are "fake" diamonds different from "real" diamonds? How are they the same?**

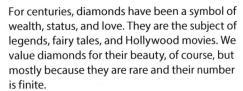

REAL FAKE DIAMONDS

For centuries, diamonds have been a symbol of wealth, status, and love. They are the subject of legends, fairy tales, and Hollywood movies. We value diamonds for their beauty, of course, but mostly because they are rare and their number is finite.

The diamond in a ring today was formed millions of years ago. Deep inside the earth, under conditions of extreme heat and pressure, carbon was pressed and cooked into the hardest of minerals. Powerful eruptions – bigger than any current volcano could produce – brought them to the surface. The conditions necessary to create diamonds no longer exist naturally, but they can be simulated in a lab. Instead of millions of years, man-made diamonds can be created in about a month.

Chemically, man-made diamonds are exactly the same as natural diamonds: They are 100% carbon, formed by high heat and immense pressure. They look identical, too. Even professional jewelers have a hard time telling them apart. In fact, the only real difference is history. For some people, however, history matters. A natural diamond has flaws that make it imperfect but also unique. Man-made diamonds are "too perfect."

Man-made diamonds have advantages over natural ones, beyond their lower price (usually about 30% less). They are not politically controversial, like the so-called "blood diamonds" of the past. Best of all, man-made diamonds can be made to order. If you want a stone of a particular size and with a slight pink color, you don't have to search the world for it. Just tell the manufacturer when you place your order. In a few weeks, you'll have your own personalized real fake diamond.

B **UNDERSTAND WORDS IN CONTEXT** **Read the article again. Then <u>underline</u> the correct definitions of the words.**

1 beyond: *more than just / related to*

2 finite: *limited / unlimited*

3 flaw: *big difference / error or imperfection*

4 mineral: *a type of stone, like marble or coal / an element, like carbon or oxygen*

5 pressure: *space / force*

6 simulate: *to prove the accuracy of / to copy or recreate*

2 CRITICAL THINKING

A **THINK CRITICALLY** **Would you say that man-made diamonds are fake diamonds? Why or why not? Imagine you wanted to buy a piece of diamond jewelry today. Would you choose natural or man-made diamonds? Why? Give at least three reasons to explain your preference.**

3 WRITING

A **Read the review about a face product. Does it sound fake? Would you want to try it? Why or why not? Underline the language used to persuade.**

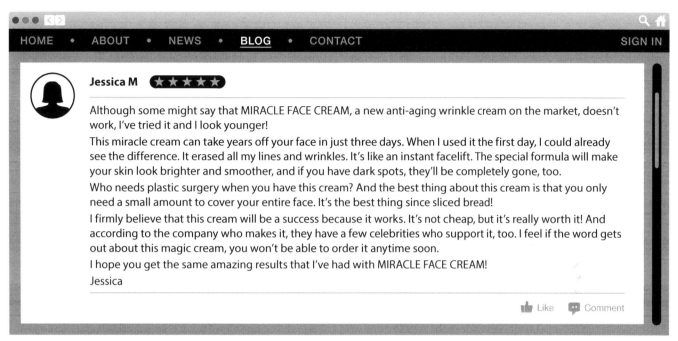

Jessica M ★ ★ ★ ★ ★

Although some might say that MIRACLE FACE CREAM, a new anti-aging wrinkle cream on the market, doesn't work, I've tried it and I look younger!

This miracle cream can take years off your face in just three days. When I used it the first day, I could already see the difference. It erased all my lines and wrinkles. It's like an instant facelift. The special formula will make your skin look brighter and smoother, and if you have dark spots, they'll be completely gone, too.

Who needs plastic surgery when you have this cream? And the best thing about this cream is that you only need a small amount to cover your entire face. It's the best thing since sliced bread!

I firmly believe that this cream will be a success because it works. It's not cheap, but it's really worth it! And according to the company who makes it, they have a few celebrities who support it, too. I feel if the word gets out about this magic cream, you won't be able to order it anytime soon.

I hope you get the same amazing results that I've had with MIRACLE FACE CREAM!

Jessica

👍 Like   💬 Comment

B **USE PERSUASIVE LANGUAGE Read the review again. Choose a product below and write a review with a strong opening sentence that gives the opposite opinion first. Use persuasive language.**

hair thickener	nail polish	shampoo for dry hair
shaving cream	sunglasses	toothpaste whitener

CHECK AND REVIEW

Read the statements. Can you do these things?

UNIT 11	Mark the boxes. ☑ I can do it. ? I am not sure. **I can …**		If you are not sure, go back to these pages in the Student's Book.
VOCABULARY	☐ describe fake goods. ☐ talk about untrue information.		page 108 page 110
GRAMMAR	☐ use passive forms. ☐ use passive with modals and modal-like expressions, and passive infinitives.		page 109 page 111
LISTENING AND SPEAKING SKILLS	☐ listen for specific information. ☐ express belief and disbelief.		page 112 page 113
READING AND WRITING SKILLS	☐ work out meaning from context. ☐ write a persuasive essay.		page 114 page 115

12.1 PRACTICE MAKES PERFECT

1 VOCABULARY: Skill and performance

A Complete the sentences with the words in the box.

analytical	artistic	athletic	competent	~~determined~~
gifted	imaginative	intellectual	logical	musical
skilled	talented	technical	trained	

1 Sebastian was _____determined_____ to finish his medical degree to become a doctor.
2 I like romantic or funny movies, nothing too _____. I don't want to think too hard.
3 He's very _____ in the arts and will likely be famous one day.
4 Her _____ abilities show in every soccer game.
5 If I had any _____ ability, I'd make a painting for this wall.
6 It was the _____ thing to do in order to save time and money.
7 Luciana is not a/an _____ musician. She has just begun to play the guitar.
8 He hasn't shown himself to be very _____ at his job.
9 You have a/an _____ mind, so writing a story will be easy for you.
10 He has always been naturally _____, even from an early age.
11 She wasn't _____ properly to do this type of job.
12 I wish I could sing, but I have no _____ ability at all.
13 You need to have _____ and _____ skills if you want to be an engineer.

2 GRAMMAR: Adverbs with adjectives and adverbs

A Underline the adverb that provides more detail about the adjective or adverb in the sentence. Circle the modified word and identify it as *Adj.* (Adjective) or *Adv.* (Adverb) next to each sentence.

1 She became <u>amazingly</u> (quick) at solving math problems. _Adj_
2 Some children are exceptionally bright. _____
3 I think she is really funny. _____
4 He picked up the baby extremely gently. _____
5 It'll sell especially well just by word of mouth. _____
6 Learning a new language never came particularly easily to me. _____
7 Can I be brutally honest with you? _____
8 Henry did a fairly good job on his English test. _____

B **Add more detail to each sentence by adding the adverb in parentheses.**

1 I thought she looked beautiful when she walked down the aisle. (amazingly)

   I thought she looked amazingly beautiful when she walked down the aisle.

2 But it's not true. (necessarily)

3 It's supposed to be cloudy tomorrow. (partly)

4 I'm excited about going backstage after the concert. (especially)

5 They weren't interested in buying the house, but they said they'd think about it. (particularly)

6 There was enough food in the cupboards. (barely)

7 There's plenty of food leftover after dinner. (always)

8 He walked quickly down the street. (rather)

3 GRAMMAR AND VOCABULARY

A **Write sentences using your own ideas and the word prompts.**

1 exceptionally / athletic

   She's exceptionally athletic when it comes to sports .

2 amazingly / intellectual

   .

3 especially / logical

   .

4 hardly / trained

   .

5 extremely / gifted

   .

6 particularly / musical

   .

B **Complete the sentences so that they are true for you. Use an adverb to modify the adjectives.**

1 I think I'm skilled at _____ .

2 I don't think I'm imaginative when it comes to _____ .

3 I'm competent at _____ .

4 When I was younger, I was talented at _____ .

5 I'm determined to _____ .

1 VOCABULARY: Describing emotional impact

A   (Circle) the correct word(s) in each sentence.

1   He tried to (*raise her spirits*) / *ruin her day* by taking her out to a fancy restaurant.

2   All this extra work is going to *make my day / stress me out*.

3   I need to *take my mind off of this matter / raise somebody's spirits* for a while and just relax.

4   Taking a vacation right now might *make your day / do you good*.

5   The books he writes *capture the imagination of children / are a real downer* all over the world.

6   He *brightens up / gets down* just thinking about his boring job.

7   She *ruined my day / put my mind at rest* when she walked away without apologizing.

8   The memory of this vacation will *do me good / leave a lasting impression on me*.

9   Finding $10 on the bus today really *took my mind off / brightened up* my day.

10   Rainy days can *stress me out / be a real downer*. They make everything look so gray.

11   It *captured her imagination / made her day* when her best friend called.

12   Once you know the reason, you can relax and *brighten up / put your mind at rest*.

B   Complete the sentences using phrases from exercise 1A . More than one answer can be correct for some sentences.

1   When my friend is down, I _____brighten up_____ her day with some chocolate ice cream.

2   Traffic in the morning can really _____ when I'm trying to get to work on time.

3   Taking the afternoon off to enjoy the sunny weather might _____ .

4   Seeing him cry can _____ for me.

5   Knowing Adam was safe at home _____ .

6   Her incredible story has _____ .

7   I need to leave the office for a while and _____ work.

8   The flowers he sent _____ .

2 GRAMMAR: Making non-count nouns countable

A   Complete the sentences with an expression in the box.

a bunch of	~~a cup of~~	a piece of	a slice of	piece of	work of

1   Do you want to have _____a cup of_____ tea before you go?

2   She had _____ lemon pie for dessert.

3   This sculpture is a real _____ art.

4   I listened to a wonderful _____ music when I was at her house.

5   She bought _____ stuff at the store.

6   My professor gave me _____ advice about my future goals.

B   **Correct the mistake(s) in each sentence. Then <u>underline</u> the expression that makes the non-count noun countable.**

1   Everyone should show <u>a little bits of</u> kindness to their neighbors.

2   I heard a great pieces of advice on the radio today.

3   I had a slice of cake and two cup of coffee for lunch today.

4   There was a bunches of newspaper on the table.

5   Ariana and her friends played a games of cards at the party.

6   Would you like a slices of cheese on your hamburger?

7   Can I have two piece of bread with my dinner?

3   GRAMMAR AND VOCABULARY

A   **Write sentences using your own ideas and the word prompts. Make the non-count nouns countable.**

1   coffee / brighten up sth

   He brightened up my day when he bought me a cup of coffee   .

2   music / capture sb's imagination

   _____ .

3   kindness / make sb's day

   _____ .

4   advice / raise sb's spirits

   _____ .

5   chess / take sb's mind off sth

   _____ .

6   art / leave a lasting impression on sb

   _____ .

7   cake / do sb good

   _____ .

B   **THINK CRITICALLY** In your opinion, what are some things we could do to make someone's day positive? What are some things that might make someone's day negative?

1   LISTENING

A   🔊 **12.01**   **Listen to the conversation. Match each statement.**

1	Work	_d_	**a**	can teach you how to write.
2	Develop		**b**	the love of it.
3	There are many websites that		**c**	technical skills.
4	There are a lot of workshops		**d**	hard.
5	Write for		**e**	you'll be successful at it.
6	Enjoy it and		**f**	you can take.

B   🔊 **12.01**   **LISTEN FOR CONTRASTING IDEAS**   **Listen to the conversation again. Are the ideas optimistic or cautious? Write O or C next to each one.**

1   I can't say for certain that all these imaginative stories in my head will turn into books.   _C_

2   But I'm confident that one day it'll happen.

3   I saw no reason why I couldn't.

4   There was no guarantee that it would happen.

5   There's no harm in trying to learn how to write.

6   Well, things might not go as planned.

2   CRITICAL THINKING

A   **THINK CRITICALLY**   **Do you think Valeria has the right attitude to become a famous author? Why or why not?**

SPEAKING

A **Complete the expressions with a word from the box. Then put them in the correct columns.**

| certain | confident | guarantee | harm | planned | ~~reason~~ |

1 I see no _____reason_____ why (I can't).
2 I can't say for _____ .
3 I will do this. I'm _____ that …
4 I realize that things might not go as _____ .
5 There's no _____ in trying.
6 There's no _____ that …

Expressing optimism	Expressing caution
I see no reason why (I can't.)	

B **For each situation, complete responses to express both optimism and caution. Use expressions from 3A.**

1 Can you help me move some boxes this weekend?
   A _I see no reason why I can't. I'm not working_ .
   B _I can't say for certain, but I might be working_ .

2 I'd love to travel there one day.
   A _____ .
   B _____ .

3 My dream scenario would be to have my own business.
   A _____ .
   B _____ .

4 Can we try to get tickets to the game on Saturday?
   A _____ .
   B _____ .

5 My ultimate goal next year is to become a music teacher at this school.
   A _____ .
   B _____ .

95

1 READING

A Do you think working as an actress is fun and exciting? Read the article. Was your prediction correct? What was the day like for the actress?

Life as an actress

By Mariel van White

Yesterday, I had the opportunity to spend the day with an amazingly talented actress, Ashley Stone. And from what I experienced, being an actress not only takes a lot of skill, but determination and patience, too.

As soon as she arrived to work, at 6.00 a.m., she got checked for hair, makeup, and wardrobe. These things need to be perfect when the camera is rolling. After that, she checked in with the assistant director to make sure there hadn't been any changes to her lines. There had—and it seems there are script changes most days—so she had to memorize them before she was called in front of the cameras.

When Ashley got to the set, the director and crew were busy setting up the scene with special lights and checking camera angles. She stood around waiting, and waiting … and then, when it was time to step in front of the cameras, someone had to adjust her makeup while the wardrobe assistant checked her outfit, again!

After an *exceptionally* long time, she got to say her lines. But right in the middle of them, the director shouted "Cut!" Something wasn't perfect. It was a missing light. There are little problems like this all the time on a movie set. Ashley just had to go back to her trailer to practice her lines again. When all the actors were called back to the set, the scene was shot before another break, this time for lunch. After lunch, Ashley and the other actors spent the rest of the day shooting scenes and rehearsing for the next day. Finally, but not until 10.00 p.m., someone called it a wrap— time for everyone to go home.

Fun? It certainly didn't seem like it. There was a lot of standing around. You need to be extremely focused and patient. That's part of what acting is all about. But Ashley told me it's worth it in the end because when the film is released, millions of people around the world will see her work on the big screen.

B **UNDERSTAND CAUSE AND EFFECT** Read again. What is/was the result of each of these events?

1 The actress arrived to work.

2 The assistant director changed the lines.

3 There was a missing light.

4 Actors were called back to the set.

5 Someone called it a wrap.

6 The film is released.

2 CRITICAL THINKING

A **THINK CRITICALLY** Make a list of some other jobs that might seem exciting and fascinating, like an actor's. Choose one and think about what the reality of the job might be like.

3 WRITING

A   **Read Amelia's review of a movie. Did she like it? Why or why not? <u>Underline</u> words that show reasons or results.**

Reply Forward

To: Christian
From: Amelia
Subject: Favorite Movies

Hi Christian,

I just got back from seeing the sequel to *After the Attack*. I know the first one was one of your favorite movies. But this one was really bad, so don't waste your time!

The special effects were done exceptionally well, but the dialogue and plot were too simple. It felt like it was made for kids, so I got bored halfway through. The acting was OK, but because of the unknown actors, I wasn't connecting to anyone. There was some beautiful scenery which was as impressive as the special effects, but nothing like the first movie. The scenes were too long and drawn out; consequently, I fell into a deep sleep.

Anyway, I thought I'd save you some money!

Can't wait to see you this weekend!

Amelia

B   **SHOW REASON AND RESULT** Think about a movie you liked or didn't like. Write a review of it using words such as *so, therefore, as a result,* and *consequently.*

_____

_____

_____

_____

_____

_____

CHECK AND REVIEW

Read the statements. Can you do these things?

UNIT 12	Mark the boxes. ☑ I can do it. ? I am not sure.	If you are not sure, go back to these pages in the Student's Book.
	I can …	
VOCABULARY	☐ talk about talents and skills.	page 118
	☐ describe how to make life better.	page 120
GRAMMAR	☐ use adverbs with adjectives and adverbs.	page 119
	☐ make non-count nouns countable.	page 121
LISTENING AND SPEAKING SKILLS	☐ describe your ambitions.	page 122
	☐ express optimistic and cautious opinions.	page 123
READING AND WRITING SKILLS	☐ understand cause and effect.	page 124
	☐ write a review of a performance.	page 125

7.5 TIME TO SPEAK Negotiate for a price

A   Look for three to five items in your home that you no longer want. Answer the questions below for each item.

> ■ What makes the item worth selling?
> ■ What would be the highest price you would want to get for it?
> ■ What would be the lowest price you would sell it for?

B   Take your list of items to your next class. Bring photos of the items if you can. Negotiate and bargain for a price for other items in the classroom and for the items you are selling.

8.5 TIME TO SPEAK Make a podcast on ways to reduce stress

A   Think of the last time you were really stressed. Make notes. Use the questions below to help you.

> ■ What were you stressed about?
> ■ What action or actions did you take to reduce the stress?
> ■ Was this action simple and effective?

B   Share what happened and what you did in your next class.

9.5 TIME TO SPEAK Talk about key events in your life

A   Think of important or interesting things you've done or experienced in the past five years. Use the questions below to help you.

> ■ What have I done or experienced?
> ■ What have I been doing in my free time?
> ■ Do I have any regrets?
> ■ Have my relationships been good or bad?
> ■ Where have I traveled/worked?

B   Share your list and then listen to a partner's list. Make positive comments about good things you hear and reassuring comments about not-so-good things.

10.5 TIME TO SPEAK Attracting talent

A   Go online and find three companies where experienced and talented employees would want to work. Use the questions below to help you.

> ■ Who are they?
> ■ What do they do?
> ■ Why would employees like to work for them?
> ■ What makes their websites attractive?

B   Create a presentation about your companies and bring it to your next class. What company would your class like to work for the most? What about the least? Ask the class to give you reasons.

11.5 TIME TO SPEAK Does it really work?

A   Think of a tip that you might follow when you are sick with a cold or flu. Use the questions below to help you.

- What is the tip?
- Where did you find it?
- What do you have to do?
- How effective is it?

B   In your next class, present your tip to the class. As a class, choose the tips you believe will be the most effective.

12.5 TIME TO SPEAK Me, in two minutes

A   Go online and research someone famous with a special talent. Use the questions below to help you.

- What skills does/did the person have?
- Was the person born gifted or trained?
- What has the person done?

B   In your next class, pretend you are this person. Describe your talents and abilities for about two minutes to the class. The class then asks questions to find out who you are.

The authors and publishers acknowledge the following sources of copyright material and are grateful for the permissions granted. While every effort has been made, it has not always been possible to identify the sources of all the material used, or to trace all copyright holders. If any omissions are brought to our notice, we will be happy to include the appropriate acknowledgments on reprinting & in the next update to the digital edition, as applicable.

Key: U = Unit.

Text

U9: Daniel Wendler for the adapted text from 'The Secret Of Conversation Flow', https://www.improveyoursocialskills.com/conversation/conversation-flow. Copyright © Daniel Wendler. Reproduced with kind permission. **U10:** The Professional Writer for the adapted text from 'How to write a Company Profile that wins business' by LYNDALL. Copyright © The Professional Writer. Reproduced with kind permission of Lyndall Guinery-Smith.

Photographs

The following photographs are sourced from Getty Images.

U7: Westend61; LenaSkor/iStock/Getty Images Plus; blue jean images; Anfisa Kameneva/EyeEm; claudio.arnese/E+; Maskot; Tim Robberts/Taxi/Getty Images Plus; **U8:** Kathleen Finlay/Image Source; Westend61; skynesher/E+; FangXiaNuo/E+; WHL; **U9:** sturti/E+; Neustockimages/E+; Deagreez/iStock/Getty Images Plus; Maskot; bernardbodo/iStock/Getty Images Plus; **U10:** Eugenio Marongiu/Cultura; Hero Images; PeopleImages/E+; F.J. Jiménez/Moment; MangoStar_Studio/iStock/Getty Images Plus; mustafagull/E+; Petardj/iStock/Getty Images Plus; John Harper/Moment; levente bodo/Moment; pixelfit/E+; skynesher/E+; gradyreese/E+; **U11:** JAY DIRECTO/AFP; mustafagull/E+; Strauss/Curtis; Mihajlo Maricic/EyeEm; World Perspectives/Photographer's Choice/Getty Images Plus; Photographer is my life/Moment; mevans/E+; **U12:** andresr/E+; Michael Blann/DigitalVision; Hinterhaus Productions/Taxi/Getty Images Plus; Chaiyaporn Baokaew/Moment; Westend61; Paolo Sartori; Yurdakul/E+.

Front cover photography by Hans Neleman/The Image Bank/Getty Images Plus/Getty Images.

Typeset by emc design ltd.

Audio

Audio production by CityVox, New York.

URL

The publisher has used its best endeavors to ensure that the URLs for external websites referred to in this book are correct and active at the time of going to press. However, the publisher has no responsibility for the websites and can make no guarantee that a site will remain live or that the content is or will remain appropriate.

Corpus

Development of this publication has made use of the Cambridge English Corpus (CEC). The CEC is a multi-billion word collection of contemporary spoken and written English. It includes British English, American English, and other varieties. It also includes the Cambridge Learner Corpus, the world's biggest collection of learner writing, developed in collaboration with Cambridge Assessment. Cambridge University Press uses the CEC to provide evidence about language use that helps to produce better language teaching materials. Our Evolve authors study the Corpus to see how English is really used, and to identify typical learner mistakes. This information informs the authors' selection of vocabulary, grammar items and Student's Book Corpus features such as the Accuracy Check, Register Check, and Insider English.

This page is intentionally left blank